PRO WRESTLING LEGENDS

Steve Austin
The Story of the Wrestler They Call "Stone Cold"

Bill Goldberg

Bret Hart
The Story of the Wrestler They Call "The Hitman"

The Story of the Wrestler
They Call "Hollywood" Hulk Hogan

Randy Savage
The Story of the Wrestler They Call "Macho Man"

The Story of the Wrestler They Call "Sting"

The Story of the Wrestler They Call "The Undertaker"

Jesse Ventura
The Story of the Wrestler They Call "The Body"

CHELSEA HOUSE PUBLISHERS

PRO WRESTLING LEGENDS

The Story of the Wrestler They Call "Sting"

Kyle Alexander

Chelsea House Publishers
Philadelphia

Produced by Choptank Syndicate, Inc.

Editor and Picture Researcher: Mary Hull
Design and Production: Lisa Hochstein

CHELSEA HOUSE PUBLISHERS

Editor in Chief: Stephen Reginald
Managing Editor: James D. Gallagher
Production Manager: Pamela Loos
Art Director: Sara Davis
Director of Photography: Judy L. Hasday
Senior Production Editor: LeeAnne Gelletly
Cover Illustrator: Keith Trego

Cover Photos: WCW
     Jeff Eisenberg Sports Photography

The Chelsea House World Wide Web site
address is http://www.chelseahouse.com

3 5 7 9 8 6 4 2

Library of Congress Cataloging-in-Publication Data

Alexander, Kyle
   The story of the wrestler they call Sting / Kyle Alexander
     p. cm.— (Pro wrestling legends)
   Includes bibliographical references (p.) and index.
   Summary: A biography of Steve Borden, the professional wrestler known as
Sting.
   ISBN 0-7910-5405-5 (hard.)— ISBN 0-7910-5551-5 (pbk.)
   1. Sting (Wrestler), 1959– Juvenile literature. 2. Wrestlers—United States—
Biography—Juvenile literature. [1. Sting (Wrestler), 1959– . 2. Wrestlers.]
I. Title. II. Series.
GV1196.S75A54 1999
796.812'092— dc21
[B]   98-34305
                      CIP

Contents

MISTAKEN IDENTITY

I t rained on that September day in 1996. The hard, driving downpour seemed endless as it cast gloom over a World Championship Wrestling (WCW) *Monday Nitro* television broadcast.

Not that the wrestling promotion had not experienced its own share of gloom, if not impending doom. The New World Order (NWO), just a few months old, had caused a great deal of strife and havoc for everyone.

After the formation of the NWO, wrestlers from outside and inside WCW were being recruited to join "Hollywood" Hulk Hogan and his contingent of rulebreakers with attitude. Paranoia ruled.

NWO limousines were parked outside the arena. There was a great bustle of activity with members of the renegade organization entering and leaving the building. The NWO was up to something, but what? During the live broadcast, a television camera taped Ted DiBiase talking into the window of one of the limousines. The window was tinted black, so the occupant could not be seen. The voice, however, was very familiar.

"I'm tired of this stuff," said the nervous individual inside the car. "This D.T.A. stuff. Don't trust anybody. It's got to go.

The NWO had everyone convinced that Sting had joined their ranks in the fall of 1996. WCW wrestlers, including his closest friends, were sure that Sting had turned to the dark side. But someone else was behind that face paint.

You know why? You better learn to trust some-body right now."

Lex Luger thought the voice sounded familiar as well. The "Total Package" was watching the startling scene from a monitor in the dressing room. He needed to resolve the doubt in his mind that was forcing him to think the worst of his best friend, Sting.

Yes, it was Sting's voice that came out of that limousine. Sting, the man who had captured the hearts of millions of fans worldwide. Sting, the man who had won four prestigious *Pro Wrestling Illustrated* magazine Most Popular Wrestler of the Year Awards.

Sting, the last man anyone thought would join the NWO.

Luger ran out to the rain-soaked parking lot in the hopes of confronting DiBiase and the mystery man. As he walked towards the limousine, DiBiase stood in front of him. Luger asked where Sting was. DiBiase looked confused.

Suddenly, out of the vehicle came a figure wearing a white trenchcoat. His hair was brown and his face was decorated with face paint.

Sting!

Luger was stunned. There he was, face-to-face with his best friend—who had just come out of an NWO limousine. Sting immediately attacked Luger, punching him mercilessly until Luger fell to the ground, then kicking him relentlessly while DiBiase cheered on every blow.

The fans watching on the arena monitors and on their home television sets were shocked. The announcers struggled to find words to describe what was happening. The emotion showed in their voices.

"No! No! Sting has turned!" cried WCW television announcer Eric Bischoff who, at that time, had yet to turn his back on WCW and join the NWO.

"He's been bought off by DiBiase!" said commentator Mike Tenay.

The timing could not have been any worse. Fall Brawl, WCW's annual September pay-per-view event, was only six days away. Sting was on the roster of Team WCW that was slated to face Team NWO in a match of great significance that would determine the balance of power between these two groups.

Representatives of both groups would battle in a "War Games" bout, a contest with a reputation for violence as two teams of four men enter side-by-side rings enclosed in a steel cage, one by one every two minutes. When all eight men are in the cage, the team that can force one member of the opposing team to submit wins.

To lose one member to the other side greatly affects that team's chances for victory. For WCW, it was a devastating turning point in their war with the NWO. Sting, so loyal to WCW for so many years, had abandoned them for the enemy.

Or had he?

On the day of the match, Sting confronted his teammates Lex Luger, Ric Flair, and Arn Anderson while they were being interviewed on television. Luger would not allow Sting to say a word. He had to at least speak first.

"I've been waiting six days for this," said Luger glaring at his "friend." "I've got to hear this. But you better make this short and sweet."

Friends Lex Luger and Sting pose with 11-year-old Ryan Loepke at a fund-raising event for the Childhood Cancer Foundation. In September 1996 Luger was stunned by the possibility that his friend Sting had turned on him and joined the NWO. To his relief, he later discovered it wasn't true.

"I'll make it real short," responded Sting in a desperate attempt to defend himself. "All I've got to say is it was not me on Monday night. It wasn't me, Lex!"

"I saw you. I looked you right in the face before you cheap-shotted me," a doubting Luger shot back at Sting. "Stinger, I know it was you. I can't believe you, and I don't believe you."

There was little more that Sting could say to ease Luger's doubts, "If you can't believe me, then so be it. I'll see you in a while," Sting said as he left the interview area.

As the War Games main event was set to begin, fans and friends of Sting anxiously waited to get their first glimpse of the popular wrestler on the side of the NWO. The shock of seeing Sting attacking Luger was still fresh in everyone's minds. The balance of power seemed to be shifting away from WCW.

The much-anticipated match was underway as Team WCW squared off against Team NWO. The crowd was focused on the match, but would occasionally look over at the entrance-way. They were waiting for Sting to emerge.

Another two-minute threshold in the bout had been reached, and it came time for the NWO to bring another man from the dressing room into the fray. Out walked a tall, muscular brunette wearing black and white face paint. There were no cheers at first when he strode to the ring. Then the jeers and catcalls started to fill the arena. Sting, of all people, was being booed!

He entered the cage and immediately attacked Team WCW with anger and intensity. At first, Sting's friends didn't know how to combat their now-former friend. They were hesitant to return the physical assault; it just didn't seem right.

The NWO had all their men in the cage as they continued to punish the wrestlers representing WCW, who found themselves one man short. How would they survive the onslaught? Who could possibly save them now?

Suddenly and surprisingly, WCW's fourth man appeared in the arena to even the odds. It was Sting!

Sting?!

The man pushed aside the curtain and sprinted to the ringside area. Same brown hair, same black and white face paint. One was clearly an impostor, but which one? Was this all another NWO scheme?

When the new combatant entered the ring, he made his true identity clear. He dominated the NWO with punches, chops, and "Stinger splashes," brutal clotheslines into the corner turnbuckles. The moves and the warrior's yell to the crowd erased all doubt in anyone's mind: the real Sting had arrived. He had been telling the truth earlier. He wasn't in the limousine six nights earlier.

Then who was?

Sting was never even close to the arena that night. He had taken a night off to rest and relax after a flight from Los Angeles to Atlanta. Little did he know that his brief vacation would cause such strife and tension in both his professional and personal lives.

The real Sting could only watch the live *Nitro* broadcast helplessly as the announcers were offering their reactions to his betrayal. For so many years, Sting brought cheers from all the fans in the arena. On that night, Sting drew boos for the first time since he was a rookie. His popularity had ended with one punch to Lex Luger. How interesting that he was not even there to experience it.

Initially, Sting desperately wanted to contact his friends and clear up the confusion. But the more he heard the words of hatred and disgust directed at him, the more he resisted placing that important telephone call. He made a decision to stay home while the events continued on without him. Perhaps he was hoping that those who questioned him would remember his track record. That didn't happen, however, which is probably what hurt Sting the most.

Now, during War Games, it was time for Sting to make the impostor hurt at least as much. The fans cheered on their hero as Sting continued his brutal assault, and his teammates (who must have been embarrassed by their doubts) cheered him on to hopeful victory. Now WCW had a chance to win this important match!

Then Sting stopped his attack and moved toward the door of the cage. Before he took another step, he turned to his friend, Lex Luger.

"Is that good enough for you right there?" an emotional Sting asked his longtime partner, referring to his ferocious attack on the NWO. "Is that proof enough?"

He walked out of the cage and left the ringside area, disappearing back through the entryway to the dressing room. Sting had not come to the War Games match to win, but to teach his teammates a painful lesson: trust your friends in your heart, no matter what your eyes may see. Rely on your partners and ignore your suspicions.

WCW would go on to lose War Games and significant ground in their interpromotional war with the NWO. But the pain that Luger, Flair, Anderson, and the rest of WCW felt after the defeat could not compare to the internal suffering that Sting was experiencing. After all he had done on behalf of WCW—"carrying the ball" is how Sting would describe it—his fellow wrestlers quickly passed judgment on his character. The wounds left by those accusations and assumptions were deep, and too much to bear.

Sting changed on that night. He was no longer the man who had won the hearts of millions, no longer the athlete whose charisma and style commanded respect. He was, in every sense of the word, a loner.

It was a stark contrast to the Sting that everyone had known before . . . or the Steve Borden that close friends had known before the fans ever heard of a man named Sting.

2   A MAN CALLED STING

Even before he became the professional wrestler known worldwide as Sting, Steve Borden had his share of success.

Born in Omaha, Nebraska, on March 20, 1959, Borden (who later moved to Venice Beach, California) had a love and natural ability for athletic competition. Throughout his school days, he was considered a natural athlete and was very active in sports.

Colleges began to notice Borden's considerable athletic abilities, and he was presented with several scholarship opportunities. Though he had many scholastic options, Borden turned down the offers to concentrate on his chosen career of bodybuilding. His passion provided him with his first fleeting taste of professional success. While he never appeared in the Mr. USA competition (he fell just one point shy of qualifying for the premiere bodybuilding event), he was nonetheless attracting a great deal of attention throughout the bodybuilding community.

It was during that time that Borden would meet three men who would be key players in his future career: Red Bastien, Rick Bassman, and Jim Hellwig.

Before turning to pro wrestling, Steve Borden was a promising young bodybuilder hoping to qualify for the Mr. USA competition. His friends convinced him to give pro wrestling a try.

Red Bastien is a legendary wrestler whose career peaked in the 1960s. He was the first to see enormous wrestling potential in the young Borden, and he convinced the budding athlete to give the pro wrestling ring a try. For two grueling months, the now-retired mat star put Borden through a daily training regimen. Wrestling would prove to be much different from bodybuilding, however, and Borden's muscles, normally reserved for flexing and posing, gave way to aches and pains.

Rick Bassman was the man who trained and managed Powerteam USA, a quartet of young wrestlers that predated current wrestling groups like the New World Order and DeGeneration X. He, too, was impressed with Borden's physical presence and natural charisma and clearly saw his potential as a superstar wrestler.

Jim Hellwig was one of Sting's Powerteam teammates and his future tag team partner. While that name may not seem familiar to most wrestling fans, Hellwig did take on another identity when the two eventually parted ways: "the Ultimate Warrior."

As a member of Powerteam USA, Borden wrestled under the name of "Flash," while Hellwig took on the name of "Justice." (The other members of the quartet, unlike Flash and Justice, did not go on to pro wrestling stardom.)

Borden and the other members of Powerteam USA debuted on November 1, 1985, in Las Vegas, Nevada. The group did not stay together long, but Borden and Hellwig found that they had a certain chemistry together that did not exist with their other teammates.

Those years were financially lean for the two young wrestlers. There were no multimillion-

Ultimate Warrior, aka Jim Hellwig, was Borden's friend and fellow wrestler in Powerteam USA, a quartet of young wrestlers. Hellwig and Borden managed to get by on the meager income they earned as new wrestlers, and in 1985 they donned face paint and formed the tag team the Blade Runners.

dollar contracts during their formative years. They had to get by on very little, and resourcefulness was the key. In an interview, Hellwig recalled a time when the two had to creatively figure out how to get their next meal.

"We had so little money when we first started training with Red Bastien, that we got caught one night in a grocery story eating Colby cheese in the aisle," recalled Hellwig. "They caught us just as we had a mouthful of that dry cheese. We both ran so far and so fast that both of us thought we were going to have to perform CPR on one another."

After Powerteam USA dissolved, Borden and Hellwig competed in Mid-South Wrestling, which would be later known as the Universal Wrestling Federation (UWF). Donning face paint, they renamed their duo the Blade Runners. Hellwig also renamed himself "Rock." Though young and inexperienced, the two muscular athletes were an intimidating presence in the ring. Sting was often referred to by ring announcers as "every man's nightmare."

In their debut as the Blade Runners, Hellwig and Borden dominated and defeated their opponents in only 45 seconds.

The Blade Runners had a very short history together. Hellwig decided to leave Mid-South and move on to a singles career in another promotion. For the first time, Steve Borden was on his own. Bastien and Bassman were long gone, and his close friend had just left to seek stardom on his own.

Borden was determined to maintain a positive attitude, but being a young rookie, he was vulnerable to the influence of others.

While Borden had always remained a sportsman who played within the rules, the dark side of professional wrestling was starting to have an influence on him. Flash was undergoing a significant attitude change that was definitely not for the better. He also chose a new name to go along with this new chapter of his career.

Sting was born.

Sting joined forces with "Hot Stuff" Eddie Gilbert, a controversial rulebreaker who was creating havoc through his violent tactics in the UWF. Gilbert persuaded Sting to join Hot Stuff International, his stable of wrestlers, which also included future WCW star Rick Steiner. Gilbert and Sting immediately targeted the UWF tag team championship, and it didn't take long before they attained their goal: Sting received his first taste of championship gold when he and Gilbert won the UWF tag team title on July 20, 1986.

However, their reign was anything but admirable. A continued use of blatantly illegal tactics caused them to be stripped of the belts about a month later. Sting and Gilbert would regain the title in a rematch, but again lose the belts within just a few weeks. Sting and Steiner would then unite to win the title back for their leader, but again the reign would be short-lived.

Sting quickly realized that illegal tactics and career shortcuts were only leading to short-term success.

Finally seeing the truth about his associates, Sting defected from Hot Stuff International and a very violent feud was born. Partners became enemies as Sting, Gilbert, and Steiner did battle in a series of singles and tag team matches.

During this wild feud, Sting was finding a new set of friends as he began receiving career guidance and moral support from wrestlers who were more interested in fair play. He was also hearing cheers for the first time in his career.

Fans were warming up to this man called Sting.

The success of the UWF caused a much larger promotion, the National Wrestling Alliance (NWA), to take notice of the smaller group. The two organizations forged a relationship and copromoted several wrestling cards (events) on which Sting was a featured competitor.

In 1987, the NWA fully absorbed the entire UWF. Sting was now a rising star in a much larger galaxy, wrestling under a bright spotlight and facing a future that was brighter still. Sting was gaining notoriety, but he was also gaining enemies, because a young, talented, and charismatic wrestler gaining momentum in his career leads to other wrestlers becoming jealous and feeling threatened.

In his first encounter with Ric Flair, the WCW World title holder, Sting was too inexperienced to prevail over the rule-breaking champion, who used illegal tactics to pin Sting.

Enter "Nature Boy" Ric Flair.

Flair had just lost his NWA World title and was obsessed with regaining it, as he had done four times before. About the same time, Sting was gaining a following that was causing the NWA promoters to take notice of this young, rising star. They saw potential in Sting and considered the money that could be generated with him in a main-event, championship match.

Blinded by paranoia and determined to regain his championship, Flair sent then-fellow Four Horsemen member Lex Luger to wrestle Sting in an effort to remove him from title contention. The Nature Boy saw Sting as another obstacle in his quest to be champion again. Luger and Sting wrestled several matches and traded victories, but no one man would be called dominant in that feud.

For Sting and Luger, it was the start of an ongoing love-hate relationship that would define a majority of their careers.

Flair, meanwhile, succeeded in recapturing the World title by defeating Ronnie Garvin at Starrcade on November 26, 1987. The event also marked Sting's pay-per-view debut as he joined Jim Garvin and Michael Hayes to compete in a six-man match against Larry Zbyszko, Eddie Gilbert, and Rick Steiner; Sting's team lost. After that card, Sting decided to make the World title his goal.

He made it clear to anyone who would listen that he wanted Flair.

A confrontation with Flair's manager, James J. Dillon, eventually persuaded the Nature Boy to give Sting a title match. Dillon confronted Sting after one of his matches, and even threw a glass of champagne into the "Stinger's" face.

This act enraged Sting and he savagely attacked the manager. For a brief time, the fury of the rulebreaking Sting emerged in an attempt to destroy Dillon.

The difference, though, was that this time the fans were solidly behind their newfound hero.

Flair, eager to avenge the attack on his manager, granted Sting a World championship match on December 12, 1987. A little more than two years after his debut, far from small arenas and stolen Colby cheese, Sting was wrestling for his first World title.

In their first encounter, Flair showed Sting what a veteran, rulebreaking champion could do to an inexperienced foe. Sting held his own with the champion, though, which only irritated the Nature Boy even more. Flair would retain the title in that match, but he did so by holding the ropes and illegally pinning Sting.

The two would meet again in February of the following year. For Sting, it was more of the same from Flair: eye gouges, punches, and chokes. Flair again kept his precious title, but after the match concluded, Sting decided to give the Nature Boy a dose of his own painful tactics. He placed Flair in his "Scorpion deathlock," a move in which he ties up the legs of the opponent, turns him over, and leans back to apply pressure on the back.

Sting had Flair in the hold for several minutes, injuring the champion and forcing him to be carried out of the arena on a stretcher.

Flair was enraged. He had held on to the belt but had been humiliated by his opponent's dominance and skills in an after-match attack. Flair needed to raise the stakes. He knew he would wrestle Sting again, but this time he wanted to do it under the bright spotlights of national television. The Nature Boy didn't just want to humble his opponent in an arena, he wanted to show the world what he could do to Sting.

Little did he know that Sting would be the one humbling his opponent.

3 BETRAYED AND INJURED

T here are certain moments that define wrestlers, that elevate mid-card grapplers forever into main event superstars, that are etched forever in the annals of wrestling history.

Such a moment came for Sting on March 27, 1988.

The NWA was airing its first Clash of the Champions, a live wrestling card televised around the world. The main event would be Sting facing World heavyweight champion Ric Flair. Due to the controversial finishes of their previous encounters, this bout would have a special stipulation.

There must be a winner.

Five judges were selected to rule on a victor in case the 45-minute time limit ended the match.

When the bell rang, the two men cautiously circled each other. As in their previous bouts, it was a contest of Flair's scientific skills and experience against Sting's brute strength and youthful exuberance. Flair immediately went for the illegal tactics to both dominate and frustrate his opponent, but Sting seemed invincible to every one of Flair's punches, chops, and kicks.

Every move from either man had a counter from the other. Sting even responded to the Nature Boy's trademark

Sting's matches with WCW heavyweight champion Ric Flair brought him national recognition, increased popularity, and respect from other wrestlers.

figure-four leglock with his own version of the crippling move.

When the bell rang again, 45 minutes had passed in a blur of wrestling maneuvers. Neither man stood out as the more dominant in the even matchup. Exhausted, both men waited for the judges to rule.

Two voted for Flair, two favored Sting, and one ruled the match a draw. Flair would hold on to the title. While a disappointed Sting would not emerge from that match with the World heavyweight title, he would receive the recognition that he had desired for so long.

The next morning, wrestling fans worldwide were talking about little else but this face-painted phenomenon who had taken the legendary Nature Boy to the limit.

Sting had not only increased his level of popularity with the fans, but also the level of respect accorded him by other wrestlers. The flamboyant, face-painted muscleman was now deemed championship material.

Wrestling titles, and Ric Flair, never strayed far from Sting's mind.

Sting spent the next year refining his developing abilities as he went after secondary and tag team titles. While elusive, gold around the waist of Sting seemed inevitable.

It took until March 31, 1989, for Sting to win his first title. He received an opportunity to wrestle for the NWA/World Championship Wrestling (WCW) television title against champion Mike Rotunda, who offered Sting the belt and $10,000 if Sting could pin him in 10 minutes.

Sting did just that.

Ironically, the path that brought him to championship gold would soon lead him back to Ric Flair.

On July 23, 1989, Sting faced Japanese superstar "The Great Muta" at the Great American Bash pay-per-view event. It was a match filled with controversy as two referees were in a conflict over the outcome. Neither man left with the belt; Muta would capture the title in a subsequent rematch.

Later that night, Flair was wrestling long-time foe and former World champion Terry Funk in the main event of the Bash. Before the show, unknown to all but Funk and Muta, a partnership had been forged. After Funk was pinned by Flair, who was now hearing his share of cheers from the fans, Muta came out to attack the Nature Boy. Still angry from their earlier encounter, Sting went out to avenge the loss of his title.

He found himself in the strange position of helping a hated foe.

Sting had Flair's attention yet again, but this time as an ally. The two called a truce. Flair was appreciative of Sting's help, so much so that the two decided to join forces and battle Funk and Muta in the main event of Halloween Havoc three months later. It was a battle that they overwhelmingly won.

An unlikely friendship was beginning.

A few weeks later, old friends of Ric Flair, Ole and Arn Anderson, returned to the NWA after a long absence. The uncle-nephew tag team had once been a part of the original "Four Horsemen" with Flair. Ole had been inactive while Arn had spent some time in the World

Wrestling Federation (WWF). All three men were looking to rekindle the past and reform the Horsemen. A fourth man would be needed.

On December 13, 1989, Starrcade, the NWA's premiere card of the year, was going to feature a four-person "Iron Man" tournament. All four men would wrestle each other in a series of one-on-one bouts and be rated on a point system. The quartet selected on that night was the Great Muta, Lex Luger, Ric Flair, and Sting.

Sting and Flair met in the final match. If Sting defeated Flair, he would win the tournament. Nearly two years after they first met, Sting finally accomplished what had eluded him for so long. He pinned the Nature Boy.

The Andersons, who had accompanied Flair to ringside, entered the ring and moved towards a jubilant Sting. The fans sensed a classic Horsemen sneak-attack, remembering heinous events of the group's early days. That would not be the case this time, though, as all three Horsemen congratulated the Iron Man.

On January 2, 1990, all four men made the union official. Sting was a Horseman.

Sting was at the peak of his career. He was a member of an elite group and he had a nontitle, pinfall victory over the NWA World heavyweight champion. While beating Flair seemed to unify Sting and the Horsemen, it would, however, eventually lead to a rift between Sting and the other men.

NWA/WCW promoters desired yet another Sting-Flair encounter. While the two stars were friends and now business associates, Sting's status as a number one contender, due to his Iron Man victory, could not be ignored. Flair was mandated to face the top contender, and that just happened to be Sting.

Sting would accept that match. After all, every wrestler's ultimate goal is to be World champion, no matter who the reigning titlist is. But with that acceptance came consequences.

When word leaked out that Sting wanted the rematch, the other three Horsemen felt betrayed. They thought Sting had traded loyalty for a title shot. Sting saw it as a professional opportunity that was not meant to mean anything personally.

The Horsemen saw that Sting had gone against their code of honor.

At a televised Clash of the Champions card on February 6, 1990, the Four Horsemen came out for an interview. It was the first opportunity that the quartet had to be featured in such a public gathering. However, it would be the last time that the four men would be allied.

Ole Anderson immediately grabbed the microphone, glared at Sting, and sternly said, "Sting, you're not going be a Horseman anymore. That's it. You're finished as a Horseman."

Sting was speechless. His mouth hung open as the words left his comrade's mouth. Anderson scolded him for taking the title shot against Flair at the upcoming pay-per-view. He told Sting that he had two hours to give up the match or his wrestling career would end on that night. They could easily take him out right there, but he was given the option of walking away unharmed.

Sting pleaded for an explanation, but Flair interrupted him. "Sting," Flair began. "I bought you a little time because of all you've done for me."

Ole interrupted him, "No, that's too easy," he said, then redirected his tirade at Sting. "You've got two hours. You're no longer a Horseman. And if we ever see you again, you're not going to be so lucky."

"Wait a minute, I don't understand," Sting protested as the Horsemen walked away. Sting reached out for his now-former partners but was met with Flair's fist to his painted face.

As the other Horsemen pinned Sting to the ropes, Flair viciously slapped him and screamed, "I tried to tell you. I bought you some time. Now do the smart thing. Smarten up. Get out of this business. Get out of our lives. You're done!"

Flair's knee connected with Sting's midsection as the ex-Horseman crumpled to the mat. The Horsemen left him lying in the ring, sparing

After Sting's victory at the NWA "Iron Man" tournament on December 13, 1989, the Horsemen invited him to join the group. However, when Sting accepted a title match against fellow Horseman Ric Flair, the group turned on him.

him from any more abuse. A chorus of boos rained down upon Flair and the Andersons as they returned to the dressing room area.

The pain Sting felt was more emotional than physical. Being slapped and kicked by Flair was painful enough, but the sense of betrayal he felt was overwhelming.

The feelings would not go unheeded.

Two hours later, the three Horsemen were wrestling the Great Muta, Dragon Master, and Buzz Sawyer in a cage match when Sting ran out to give them his answer. The truth was that Sting never considered giving up the title match with Flair. He knew what his message would be, and he knew exactly how to deliver it.

He climbed to the top of the cage.

Security officials ran out to hold back Sting and prevent a violent confrontation. They pulled Sting off the cage. Sting landed on the floor. Suddenly, he heard a pop, and a sharp pain shot through his body. He ignored it to get to Flair and his cohorts.

As he was escorted backstage, Sting realized that his weight would not support his left knee. Something was wrong. Very wrong.

After a thorough examination by a doctor, the diagnosis was given to him. Sting had suffered a tendon tear in his knee. Not only would it require major surgery, but he would not be able to wrestle for a minimum of six months.

Sting, a number one contender and a rising superstar just beginning to realize his potential, was on the sidelines, definitely for six months, perhaps for good.

The World title shot with Flair would go to someone else.

Sting's moment of glory would have to wait.

4 THE CHAMPION

Sting's knee injury was bad, but it could have been worse. He underwent successful knee surgery, but his doctor's prognosis was less than satisfying to the young wrestler. His knee would need a minimum of six months to heal. Six months away from the ring. Six months to wait for Ric Flair.

Forced to watch the action, Sting took on the role of cheerleader as Lex Luger, his closest friend, was elevated to top contender status in the WCW. On many occasions Sting accompanied Luger to watch his friend face Flair.

More often than not, his presence at ringside made him a target of attacks by the Four Horsemen. It also reminded the Horsemen that it was just a matter of time before the Stinger would return to action.

But questions lingered. Would he be the same wrestler who pinned Flair at Starrcade to become both an Iron Man and a Horseman? Would the time away from the ring have dulled Sting's sharp wrestling skills?

Knowing that Sting was on the road to recovery, the Horsemen were determined to do something about it. They mercilessly attacked him at two consecutive pay-per-view

---

Though Sting lost his hard-earned U.S. heavyweight title to Rick Rude in 1991, he refused to let any setback prevent him from winning his second WCW World championship.

shows; Sting was fortunate to escape both attacks without significant additional injury.

Sting was healing ahead of schedule, and WCW promoters were eager to sign a Sting-Flair rematch as soon as possible. After a thorough examination, his doctors proclaimed him ready for action.

The night of June 13, 1990, was a time for action.

Sting's opportunity came after Flair was disqualified in a NWA World title defense. The champion decided to run the other way and avoid any encounter with his enemy. Sting went to the ring to send a direct message to the champion.

"I want my chance so bad," yelled Sting, referring to his long-awaited title shot. "Please, I'm begging you. I don't care when. Let's sign another World title match."

Sting could not contain his enthusiasm. Being in the middle of the ring rejuvenated him. Hearing the crowd energized him. He felt their support as he continued his plea.

"It's about my time," Sting said. "I will get down on my knees and beg you. The World title means just as much to me as it does you. Probably more."

Promoters agreed and immediately responded to Sting's request. He received his long-awaited title match against Flair at WCW's premiere summer event The Great American Bash, scheduled for July 7, 1990.

As was his custom, Sting wore unique face paint for this match. Appropriately, he chose the colors red, white, and blue—to signify not just the independence of his country, but also his own independence from his injury.

Wearing red, white, and blue face paint for his long-awaited title shot, Sting puts a Scorpion death-lock on reigning WCW champion Ric Flair at the Great American Bash on July 7, 1990. Sting defeated Flair to win his first WCW World heavyweight title.

The match was another classic from these two great athletes. Again, both men were evenly matched. Flair's technical ability was countered by Sting's high-flying techniques. Would another shining moment for Sting end in a draw?

The Horsemen didn't intend to stand around and watch their leader lose. They stormed the ring to assist the Nature Boy as Sting clamped on the Scorpion deathlock. Their attempt was stopped by allies of Sting, dubbed the "Dudes with Attitudes," who battled the Horsemen outside the ring.

One way or another, Sting was determined to get a fair chance at winning the championship.

Flair tried to pin Sting with his feet on the ropes. One of the Dudes, Scott Steiner, pushed Flair's feet off to prevent a tainted win. Flair was angered at the interference but continued his assault.

In 1992 Sting challenged reigning WCW champion Lex Luger to a match that ended with Sting winning his second World heavyweight championship.

Flair tried mat wrestling to keep Sting off his feet. Sting countered perfectly. Flair chopped Sting's chest. Sting barely felt it. Sting simply could not be beaten as the crowd's support energized him even more.

The ending was remarkable in its simplicity. After two years of matches that ended in frustration, followed by five months of inactivity, followed by a cornucopia of taunts, threats, and attacks, Sting finally pinned Flair—with a simple rollup.

Sting's friends stormed the ring to embrace the new champion. He was in a state of shock. He looked at the celebrating crowd. He looked at his friends who were patting him on the back and embracing him. He was visibly moved by emotion as the referee presented him with the World title belt.

Sting savored the moment as his fans continued the celebration in the arena. He soaked in their affection, not wanting it to end. He started to walk up the ramp to the dressing room area that had brought him to the ring as a challenger less than half an hour before. A few feet from the curtain, Sting stopped and turned to face the crowd.

One last time, he acknowledged the fans who had stood by him through the most difficult time of his career. He hoisted his championship belt high in the air for all to see as the fans erupted with deafening cheers.

In the dressing room area, there was just as much pandemonium. Sting's friends circled him as reporters tried to get a quote from the new champ.

"I've said it before, but he [Flair] is the greatest World champion of all time," said a grateful and humbled Sting. "Big shoes to fill. I'm going to do the best job I can."

Not far from the celebration, the Horsemen were gathered in their dressing room. Their plan to rid the wrestling world of Sting had failed miserably. There was anger and promises of revenge.

Wrestling history has shown that while Ric Flair has lost his share of World titles, he has the ability to win them back quickly. Sting was now a target to all challengers, but those men would have to wait. Ric Flair would get the first chance.

But Flair could not get the better of Sting in their rematches. When he tired of failing, his Horsemen partners had their turns; they failed, too.

At one point, Flair tried to regain the belt by utilizing a psychological strategy, disguising himself as a masked wrestler named "the Black Scorpion" and claiming to be a mystery man from Sting's past. That bizarre plan flopped.

Under very controversial circumstances, Flair eventually won the title back on January 11, 1991. However, that setback would not stop Sting from winning more WCW championships.

In a tournament to crown a U.S. heavyweight champion, Sting defeated Steve Austin on August 25, 1991. While that victory may have been satisfying, it still was not enough for the man who had once made it to the top. The U.S. belt is viewed by many as a stepping-stone to the World title. Sting had tasted greatness; he wanted it back.

Ironically, it was on the night that he lost his U.S. title to "Ravishing" Rick Rude that Sting was put back on the title track. Lex Luger, who had won the World heavyweight championship in July, attacked his former friend and attempted to injure the knee damaged nearly two years ago. Anxious for revenge against the man he once called "partner," Sting challenged Luger for his World title.

It took Sting just one match with Luger to gain his second World title, on February 29, 1992. His reign lasted less than five months before it was ended by international superstar "Big Van" Vader. Sting won the belt back for six days in March 1993, but he had to wait more than four years before he would win the World title again.

Sting's career now, though, was about more than titles. True, championships had put Sting in the spotlight. But heated feuds with wrestling villains had brought him the affection of wrestling fans worldwide. He had become a competitor of supreme confidence, always up to any challenge, always ready to face any threat, no matter how large.

Or so he thought.

5 THE INVASION

Memorial Day is meant to be a day of remembrance. For WCW, Memorial Day 1996 was, appropriately, a day they would never forget.

During a wrestling match of little significance, an event of great significance occurred. Out from the crowd and into the ring came professional wrestler Scott Hall, fresh from competing in the rival WWF.

Hall stepped through the ropes with a microphone in his hand. He claimed that no introduction was needed; everyone knew who he was. Indeed, they did. For weeks, rumors of Hall arriving in WCW had been circulating furiously throughout the wrestling world.

When Hall spoke, the wrestling world sat up and listened—and was stunned. The man formerly known as "Razor Ramon" had declared war on WCW.

WCW wrestlers were in a state of shock. Hall was saying unspeakable things about his new home. As the weeks went on, Hall continued his threats. He raided the WCW announcing booth, frightening and driving away the commentators. He was doing everything he could do to intimidate everyone in WCW.

Sting would not be intimidated.

A determined and red-faced Sting squeezes Bill Goldberg in an immobilizing headlock during a WCW Nitro *broadcast on September 14, 1998.*

Deciding that he had heard and seen enough, Sting was the first WCW wrestler to stand up to the newcomer. The night Sting confronted Hall face-to-face, he wanted to make clear to this self-proclaimed "outsider" that he was on Sting's home turf.

"You have any idea where you are?" Sting asked forcefully. "This is WCW! You're in the jungle, baby."

Hall locked eyes with Sting, not backing down for a minute. He became more menacing as he promised Sting and WCW a "big surprise" the following week. Then, as he had done thousands of times to thousands of other wrestlers, Hall flicked his trademark toothpick at Sting. Sting answered that gesture with a slap to Hall's face.

The first shots in Hall's war with WCW had been fired.

Hall lived up to his promise and brought another ex-WWF wrestler, Kevin Nash, to assist him in his battle. Nash, a former WWF World champion under the name "Diesel," made it clear that he and Hall, now called "the Outsiders," would make an impact never before seen in WCW.

The two embarked on a WCW rampage that saw them confronting and threatening WCW wrestlers and announcers. The Outsiders were as outspoken as they were obnoxious. They wanted nothing less than complete control over WCW.

Before long, Hall and Nash began to speak of a third man who would join them in their invasion of WCW. They vowed it was a wrestler who would tip the balance of power heavily in their favor. The Outsiders demanded that WCW

In 1996 Scott Hall, aka Razor Ramon, and Kevin Nash, aka Diesel, stormed the halls of WCW, determined to gain control over the organization.

put up three of their best wrestlers so both groups could do battle in the ring.

WCW promoters, eager to quiet the Outsiders, agreed to the match and selected three of their best wrestlers to combat Hall, Nash, and their mystery man. Sting, Lex Luger, and "Macho Man" Randy Savage were chosen to represent WCW's top athletes.

As confident as "Team WCW" was, there were still serious questions about the identity of the third man. Preparation for the six-man bout was difficult, if not impossible. The secret identity of their enemy gave Hall and Nash an early advantage.

When match time arrived, Hall and Nash were still missing a third man.

Frustration set in for WCW's trio. How could Hall and Nash enter a situation where they were deliberately at a disadvantage? Something was wrong.

The match started in handicap style, with Sting, Luger, and Savage battling Nash and Hall. WCW's advantage wouldn't last as Luger

Hulk Hogan's defection to NWO in 1996 enraged Sting, who became a leading soldier in the war between WCW and the NWO.

was knocked out of the match early. Injured and unable to continue, he was carried by stretcher to the dressing room.

The match continued as a two-on-two bout, and it was particularly brutal. Sting and Savage fought bravely for WCW's sake, but the power of the seven-foot-tall Nash and his 6' 8" partner was overwhelming. Still, Sting and Savage would not surrender to the assault.

The turning point in the bout came when Sting and Hall were battling furiously outside the ring while Nash was pummeling Savage in the ring. Things did not look promising for WCW's representatives, who were on the verge of a tragic defeat.

Suddenly, a powerful figure emerged from the dressing room area.

It was Hulk Hogan.

The crowd's reaction was one of recognition and confusion. Why was he here? He had been absent for months from WCW action; why did he choose this moment to return? Of course! He was here to help Sting and Savage!

Or was he?

Nash joined Hall outside the ring as Hogan tore his shirt off, ready for a fight. Savage was prone on the mat, nearly unconscious. Celebration turned to shock as Hogan executed his trademark legdrop on Savage.

Hogan was the Outsiders's third man!

Sting tried to help his fallen partner, but was greeted with a beating from the Outsiders that knocked him back outside the ring. Sting finally pulled Savage from the ring and helped him back to the dressing room. As he took slow, painful steps, he could hear Hogan's sickening speech, telling fans to "stick it." Hogan proclaimed that he, Hall, and Nash were the New World Order of wrestling.

As the news spread throughout the wrestling world, WCW was reeling from the betrayal of their premiere athlete. Sting joined WCW in their shock. The following night, Sting was asked for his reaction to the tragic event. He spoke from the heart, a heart that was clearly broken.

"What happened last night, I am not surprised about coming from the two Outsiders," Sting said. "But, I will say I am very, very surprised at you, Hulk Hogan. I should have known when I looked into your eyes."

Sting reflected back on his time spent alongside his ally, Hulk Hogan. He claimed that there were always signs of a bitter and egotistical Hulk Hogan, but he chose to turn the other way. In a way, Sting was accepting some blame for the turn of events.

"You know something? I made a mistake. But you made a bigger mistake," Sting continued, his voice rising in anger. "Because last night, you wiped out and trashed every little kid, every single person that was a part of your life, who patterned their lives after you. You told them to say their prayers and to take their vitamins. You told them to believe in themselves.

"You know something? It's a good thing you told them to believe in themselves, because they sure as heck can't believe in you." Sting continued, knowing he no longer believed in Hogan either. "And all those little kids. You told them to stick it. No. You stick it, Hulk."

Sting hated the very words that were coming out of his mouth. Mostly because it was the truth. A painful truth. The idea of "trash talking" Hulk Hogan had been, until this moment, thoroughly unimaginable.

But Hogan was now an enemy that Sting would have to fight if WCW was to win this war against the NWO.

Sting understood the significance of his speech all too well. It was more than just a reaction to a sad chain of events. He was now carrying the banner of WCW, leading the charge against the newly formed NWO.

Sting would soon learn a painful lesson. As a leader, it is lonely at the top.

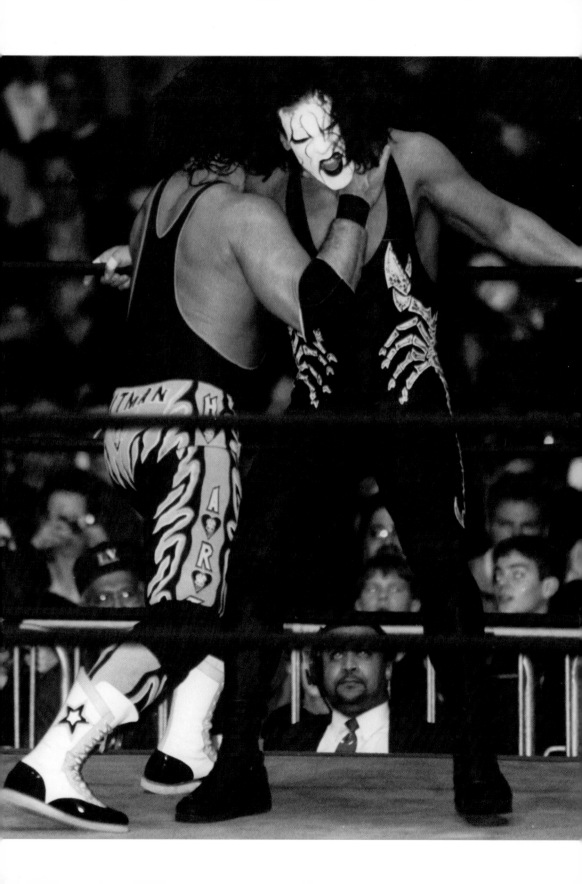

TO THE DARK SIDE AND BACK

Sting always felt that he was above reproach, that no matter what happened, his character, loyalty, and friendship would never be questioned.

From Sting's point of view, his friends should have doubted what they witnessed when "Sting"—an NWO-loyal wrestler disguised as Sting—attacked Lex Luger during the September 9, 1996, broadcast of WCW *Monday Nitro*. In the heat of the war between WCW and the NWO, however, they doubted.

And Sting—the real Sting, who confronted Luger and his WCW teammates at the Fall Brawl pay-per-view on September 15—was deeply hurt.

Sting, scheduled to be part of WCW's four-man team battling a quartet of NWO wrestlers at Fall Brawl, turned his back on WCW. It was more than just a statement of anger. It represented a deep change in his personality.

The night after Fall Brawl, Sting felt the need to speak out about what had happened over the past week. During the live WCW *Monday Nitro* broadcast, he made an unscheduled appearance in the ring to address the fans, wrestlers, and executives in WCW. With his back uncharacteristically turned away from the camera, he addressed the crowd.

Wearing the white face paint he adopted during his outcast period, a brooding Sting struggles to defend himself against Bret "Hitman" Hart.

"I carried the WCW banner. I have given my blood, my sweat, and my tears for WCW," an emotional Sting said. "So for all those fans out there, and all those wrestlers, and people that never doubted the 'Stinger,' I'll stand by you, if you stand by me."

The crowd cheered in response. Then Sting's speech took a more sinister tone.

"But, for all the people, all of the commentators, all of the wrestlers, and all of the 'best friends' who did doubt me, you can stick it," Sting pronounced. "From now on, I consider myself a free agent."

Sting had officially disassociated himself from WCW. Meanwhile, he promised the fans that they would see him again. He vowed to show up when they least expected it.

A few weeks later, the NWO formally offered him a spot with their organization. Sting turned down their request, saying that "there's only one thing for sure with the 'Stinger,' and that's that nothing is for sure."

Those words would symbolize Sting's strange journey for the next 16 months.

In the months that followed, Sting was seen lurking in the upper levels of arenas where WCW was televising their programs. The colorful face paint was gone, replaced by a ghostly-white mask. He took to wearing a long black trenchcoat and started to carry a baseball bat.

The new look was a reflection of Sting's emotional state. Sting felt betrayed by WCW. To have his motivations questioned after he had given so many years of his career to WCW was demoralizing to Sting. WCW suffered as a result. WCW's crisis with the NWO should have brought WCW's athletes closer together. Instead, Sting, their marquee man, lurked in the shadows, refusing to wrestle.

For WCW wrestlers, a normal life in the promotion had to continue, with or without Sting. They wrestled their matches and competed for titles. Were they forgetting the events that changed the promotion forever?

Sting would not let them forget. At some matches, from his place in the catwalks, Sting would rappel down to the ring, wielding a baseball bat. The first time he did, he confronted his best friend, Lex Luger, who was stunned at the new appearance of his longtime partner. Sting handed Luger his baseball bat and left in silence.

Everyone, including Luger, was confused. The significance of that moment was a mystery to all except Sting.

Sting returned to a small amount of ring activity directed at WCW wrestlers. Jeff Jarrett was the first to feel Sting's new maneuver called the "Scorpion deathdrop," a move in which he would grab a wrestler from behind by the neck and drop his body to the mat. Rick Steiner accused Sting of being anti-WCW and received a deathdrop for his comments.

For Sting, his attacks were not about taking sides. They were a not-so-gentle reminder to WCW stars that they should never let their guard down, no matter who was lurking in the shadows. It could be friend. It could be foe. The key was to keep alert at all times.

A good lesson, but the nagging question remained. Where were Sting's loyalties?

Weeks grew into months. Sting was still silent. His hair was growing longer and his mood was growing darker. Sting remained grim-faced and silent.

Nearly six months after his last words in the ring, Sting shocked the wrestling world by making an appearance in the ring wearing an NWO T-shirt. The NWO was ecstatic! Sting joining them was another step toward success in their plan to dominate WCW! What the NWO didn't know was that Sting had a plan of his own.

Uncensored on March 16, 1997, was to be Sting's first pay-per-view as an official member of the NWO. Three teams of four men each were to battle in the main event. One team was comprised of WCW stars, one of NWO stars, and one of wrestlers loyal to wrestling legend "Rowdy" Roddy Piper. While not on the team that the NWO sent into action, surely Sting would be making an appearance.

As expected, Sting dropped from the ceiling during the bout as the NWO rejoiced and

Jeff Jarrett was the first wrestler to experience Sting's new Scorpion death-drop. Sting grabbed Jarrett from behind by the neck and dropped his body to the mat.

encouraged him to join in the action. Suddenly, Sting began attacking the other NWO members. One deathdrop followed another as the bat-wielding, now-former NWO member went on a rampage. Everyone in the arena was cheering for Sting.

Sting turned to Lex Luger. No threatening looks. No bat. The two embraced. Sting was back in the camp of WCW. Or was he?

Weary of waiting for Sting to make a commitment, WCW started an active recruitment campaign. WCW executive committee chairman James J. Dillon appeared on television, pleading with Sting to rejoin their ranks. One by one, Dillon offered Sting men to wrestle. One by one, Sting turned the matches down with a silent shake of his head. In August 1997, Dillon confronted Sting, demanding that he reveal what he wanted above anything else.

Sting looked around the arena at the fans. One fan in particular was holding up a cardboard sign in support of Sting. He noticed the sign and asked the fan if he could show it to everyone in the arena, including James J. Dillon. The sign read: "Sting vs. Hogan."

Dillon didn't get the message. What Dillon failed to understand was that for Sting, it was more than Hogan's belt he wanted.

To make his message clear, Sting again appeared on television to tell his story and let his true desire be known. As Sting stood on the catwalk, the arena's sound system played the recorded voice of a child reading a poem. The verse summed up Sting's silence since that fateful fall night in 1996.

"When a man's heart is full of deceit it burns up, dies, and a dark shadow falls over his soul. From the ashes of a once-great man has risen a curse, a wrong that must be righted. We look to the skies for a vindicator, someone to strike fear into the black heart of the same man who created him. The battle between good and evil has begun. Against an army of shadows comes the Dark Warrior, the purveyor of good, with a voice of silence, and a mission of justice."

Sting wanted justice. Sting wanted "Hollywood" Hogan. Nothing more.

Hollywood Hogan wanted no part of Sting. If he could not have him as his ally, Hogan wanted to keep Sting as far away as possible. Even though Sting had not wrestled for 16 months, Hogan closely watched the brutality that Sting had carried out week after week. He did not want to become Sting's victim.

WCW promoters scheduled Sting's World title bout for December 28, 1997, at the Starrcade pay-per-view event. As champion, Hogan had little choice but to follow their orders. In the weeks leading up to the confrontation, though, Hogan employed a psychological strategy to distract Sting.

The NWO used life-size Sting mannequins in an attempt to show everyone what was going to happen at Starrcade. During various prominent telecasts, a "Sting" would drop from the ceiling in similar fashion to the way Sting had been confronting his foes. NWO members would then attack and obliterate the doll.

Sting was not affected. His mental focus on this chance at Hogan and redemption was total and all-consuming. That focus was evident on the night of Starrcade.

The lights flashed as Sting entered the ring. He did not run. He did not slap hands with the fans. In a very deliberate fashion, Sting slowly walked to the ring, where Hogan was already waiting. He stopped and pointed his baseball bat at the champion, signaling what was to come in their brutal encounter.

Hogan responded by waving his World title belt, taunting Sting to "come and get it."

Hogan was confident, and in one respect he had every right to be. For this match, Sting had a fair share of "ring rust" from his lack of wrestling activity. The champion, often criticized for his lack of frequent title defenses, still kept a far more active schedule than his foe.

Sting finally got his match with Hogan on December 28, 1997, and used the scorpion deathlock to subdue the World champion.

The two wrestlers met face-to-face in the middle of the ring. Hogan removed his trademark bandanna and threw it in Sting's face. Sting responded by slapping Hogan.

Sixteen months of pent-up anger had begun to seep out. The match was under way.

Hogan would do anything to deny Sting his chance at revenge. He attacked the challenger furiously, desperate to end the match early. Punches and kicks rained down on Sting. Hogan's physical assault was relentless.

Hollywood was getting the better of Sting, whether the match remained in the ring or spilled out of it. Perhaps Sting's layoff was too long. Perhaps he had rushed into a title encounter before he was ready.

It was becoming clear that Sting's battered body could not take much more.

With little warning, Hogan was able to put his boot right in Sting's face. The Stinger fell to the mat, and Hogan executed his famous leg-drop. With a handful of Sting's tights, Hogan lay on top of his fallen foe. The referee counted to three.

Hogan had pinned Sting.

As shock and disbelief filled the arena, something was missing: the bell signifying the end of the match. A ringside camera caught Bret Hart, a former WWF World champion who had just joined WCW, preventing the time-keeper from ringing the bell. Hart had refereed an earlier match and decided to use his status as an official to ensure justice for Sting.

"I said it would never happen again, and it's not going to happen again," screamed Hart, referring to a previous incident in his career where a referee took his World title away under controversial circumstances.

Hart felt that the fast count from an NWO-sympathetic referee and Hogan's tugging of Sting's tights had created a terrible injustice.

Already holding a referee's license for the night, Hart restarted the match. Hogan refused Hart's order and began to walk away from the ring. Hart took matters into his own hands and dragged the champion back into the ring to finish the battle with Sting.

Sting immediately took advantage of his renewed chance. He was energized. He howled to the crowd. He beat on his chest. The old Sting was finally reemerging after what seemed like an eternity of despair.

He immediately caught Hogan in two Stinger splashes. Dazed, Hogan collapsed to the mat where Sting put him in his Scorpion deathlock.

Hogan could not escape from the crippling hold, and Hart signaled for the bell.

Sting could once again call himself World champion! Tragedy had turned to vindication, and the fans loved it! WCW officials, though, had second thoughts.

The following night, a rematch was ordered to settle the disputed finish. But that match had an even more controversial ending. Hogan apparently beat Sting, but Sting still came out the victor.

On January 8, 1998, James J. Dillon came to a difficult decision. The WCW World title was too important to have it tainted by title matches where the outcomes were less than satisfactory. He ordered both Sting and Hogan to the ring for an important announcement.

Dillon ordered Sting to give up the World title.

Sting was shocked. Hogan was ecstatic, until he heard Dillon's verdict. The championship would be held up until a rematch decided who would get the belt.

Unable to get along with Hollywood Hogan in the NWO, Kevin Nash formed an NWO splinter group, called the Wolfpac, and managed to lure Randy Savage, Konnan, Lex Luger, and Sting into the den.

Sting was outraged. He glared at Dillon and snarled, "You've got no guts."

Then he turned to Hogan.

"And you," he said. "You're a dead man."

Sting won back the title in the February 22, 1998, rematch, but held it only until April 19, when he lost it to Randy Savage. Still the wrestling world was thrilled to have Sting back.

As Sting was putting his career back together, the NWO was falling apart at the seams. Problems between Hollywood Hogan and Kevin Nash caused a rift in the organization. Nash formed a splinter group within the NWO and named it the Wolfpac. He brought NWO members Randy Savage and Konnan with him. Lex Luger shocked WCW by joining up with the Wolfpac, too.

Luger would not be their last recruit, though. The Wolfpac wanted Sting to help them in their war against NWO Hollywood.

Sting signs autographs for his fans, who stand by him no matter what group he wrestles with or what color face paint he wears.

Sting didn't make any quick decisions. The fact that Luger had joined the group did not have much influence on Sting, at first. But the Stinger knew that he had to come to a decision sooner or later.

Weighing heavily on Sting's mind was the fact that he and "The Giant," an up-and-coming 7' 4", 500-pound WCW star, had just won the WCW World tag team title. Days before that May 17, 1998, victory over Scott Hall and

Kevin Nash, The Giant officially joined NWO Hollywood.

The Giant wanted Sting to go with NWO Hollywood. Luger wanted Sting to join the Wolfpac. A decision needed to be made.

After months of fighting the NWO both in and out of the ring, Sting finally chose sides and signed on to the Wolfpac, spurning his tag team partner in the process. Because the two tag team champions couldn't get along, WCW ordered a singles match between The Giant and Sting to determine ownership of the title. Sting won the June 14, 1998, bout and chose Wolfpac leader Kevin Nash as his championship partner.

Sting and Nash held the belts until July 20, 1998, when they were defeated by The Giant and Scott Hall. But whether Sting wears a belt or not, the important fact is that he's back in action, he's wrestling well, and the fans are loving it.

As has been the case so often in the Stinger's past, wrestling isn't just about winning titles. It's about honor and excellence, about sportsmanship and fair play, about friendships and deep bonds. The fans have stood behind Sting, and he has rewarded them with memorable matches and unending devotion. In the process he has become a remarkable hero in the annals of the mat sport.

He is Sting, and his kind only comes our way once in a lifetime.

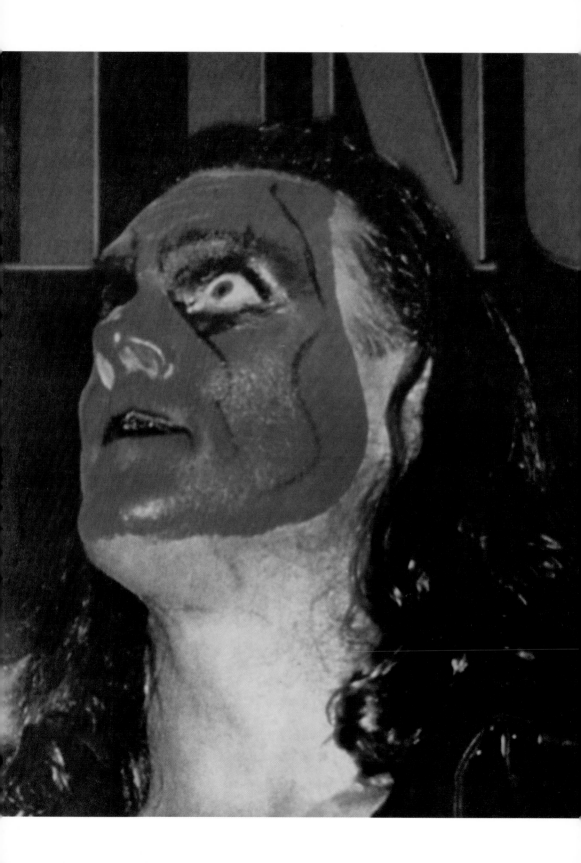

Chronology

1959   Born Steve Borden in Omaha, Nebraska, on March 20.

1985   Makes wrestling debut with Powerteam USA in Las Vegas, Nevada.

Joins Blade Runners, which debuts in Memphis, Tennessee.

1986   With Eddie Gilbert, defeats the Fantastics for the UWF tag team title.

1987   Makes NWA pay-per-view debut at Starrcade.

Wrestles Ric Flair in his first World title match.

1988   Wrestles Ric Flair to a 45-minute draw at the Clash of the Champions.

1989   Defeats Mike Rotunda for the NWA/WCW television championship.

Defeats Ric Flair in the finals of the Iron Man tournament at Starrcade.

1990   Joins the Four Horsemen.

Fired from the Horsemen and suffers a career-threatening injury.

Defeats Ric Flair for his first WCW World heavyweight title.

1991   Defeats Steve Austin in a tournament final for the U.S. championship.

1992   Defeats Lex Luger for his second WCW World title.

1996   Walks out on his War Games partners at Fall Brawl.

Announces that he is a free agent.

1997   Defeats Hollywood Hogan for a third WCW World heavyweight title.

1998   Is stripped of the WCW World title.

Regains the vacant WCW World title by defeating Hollywood Hogan.

Loses the WCW World title to Randy Savage.

With The Giant, captures the WCW World tag team title.

Defeats The Giant for ownership of the WCW World tag team title; chooses Kevin Nash as his tag team partner.

With Kevin Nash, is defeated by The Giant and Scott Hall for the WCW World tag team title.

Further Reading

Anderson, Steve. "Sting Fever Strikes: And the NWO Can't Find the Cure." *The Wrestler Digest* (spring 1998): 36–38.

Anderson, Steve. "Sting: Why the Savior of WCW Turned Out to Be the Savior of the NWO." *Pro Wrestling Illustrated* (June 1998): 40–43.

Murphy, Dan. "Now He Talks . . . but He Doesn't Say Anything: What's Really Going On in Sting's Mind?" *Pro Wrestling Illustrated* (November 1998): 19–21.

"Press Conference: Sting." *Pro Wrestling Illustrated* (January 1999): 22–23.

Rosenbaum, Dave. "Sting: He's Going to Be a Pain in the Nash." *Pro Wrestling Illustrated* (May 1999): 24–27.

Index

Photo Credits

All-Star Sports: pp. 6, 57, 58, 60; Associated Press/Wide World Photos: p. 10; Sports Action: pp. 44, 48; Jeff Eisenberg Sports Photography: pp. 14, 17, 20, 24, 30, 32, 36, 43, 52; WCW: pp. 2, 35, 40, 55.

KYLE ALEXANDER has been involved in the publication of professional wrestling magazines for a decade, both as a writer and an
illustrator. His work has been featured prominently in professional
wrestling publications all over the world. During the past 10 years, he
has made numerous appearances on radio and television, offering
his unique perspective on the "sport of kings."